the blue pearl

Born in 1958, Anne Blonstein has lived since 1983 in Basel, Switzerland, where she earns a living as a freelance translator and editor. Her poems and prose poetry have appeared in journals and anthologies in the USA, Canada, Britain, Switzerland and Austria. She has published a chapbook, *sand.soda.lime*, and collaborated with the Swiss composer, Mela Meierhans, on two works, *canthus to canthus*, and *4S*.

the blue pearl

ANNE BLONSTEIN

PUBLISHED BY SALT PUBLISHING
PO Box 937, Great Wilbraham PDO, Cambridge CB1 5JX United Kingdom
PO Box 202, Applecross, Western Australia 6153

All rights reserved

© Anne Blonstein, 2003

The right of Anne Blonstein to be identified as the
author of this work has been asserted by her in accordance
with Section 77 of the Copyright, Designs and Patents Act 1988.

This book is in copyright. Subject to statutory exception
and to provisions of relevant collective licensing agreements,
no reproduction of any part may take place without the written
permission of Salt Publishing.

First published 2003

Printed and bound in the United Kingdom by Lightning Source

Typeset in Swift 9.5 / 13

*This book is sold subject to the conditions that it shall not,
by way of trade or otherwise, be lent, re-sold, hired out,
or otherwise circulated without the publisher's prior consent
in any form of binding or cover other than that in which
it is published and without a similar condition including this
condition being imposed on the subsequent purchaser.*

ISBN 1 876857 65 X paperback

SP

1 3 5 7 9 8 6 4 2

for charles lock

Contents

the rock-that-gave-birth-to-the-sky 3
hathor in egypt 39
anilineated dreams 75

"But to Helen, to fair Helen, the beautiful, the aesthetic, the very type and first occasion of representation, no voice can be given: throughout Western history, from Homer to *Omeros*, the representation of beauty depends on a central cavernous silence. In tongueless plastic sandals lurks an echo of many scandals."

> from Charles Lock: Derek Walcott's *Omeros*: Echoes from a White-throated Vase. *The Massachusetts Review* 2000; XLI (1):28

the rock-that-gave-birth-to-the-sky

I

      "hostage to the memories of. nectar
and necklaces. isolation and island nation.
hostile witness to forgetfulness, i am speaking
she is writing. the host to fusion of planes, a joy
light and compact"

                "trail marked by sand"

                  "how to tell the stories
of the gifts, the points and the curious"

II

    "bone"

                                         "the metamorphosis of
deception as the appetite turns"

                                                        "to snakestone"

III

        "alreadyness. falling into the eyes"

                "remembering. refusing
to describe it"

                        "the cause and the barb.
                        tissue and value.
                        net in net"

IV

      "if spoken four times"

            "if summoned four times"

                  "if sung
the fourth time"

v

" "

"from stone time
to smuggled time"

"the curves return you to the polished"

VI

       "in static schemes
i know i languaged what i have spoken"

                      "so i began to take
the surface over the edges of a square"

     "and i knew i have thought what i had spoken"

VII

"a triangle holds something sacral.
frame picture. frame of vibrant extensions.
something ordered in chaos"

"frame of the bones
of bathing women. frame of pollen grains mixed with clay
water and sand. frame of oxidized silver"

"deep gray. of clouds hanging round
mountain peaks. their shadows that stroke
the snow"

VIII

        "i have always thought it means something, really gives and gets richer"

                      "i have always thought it means, and what works like the empirical?"

          "i have always thought it means that she who chose chose very wide clothes"

IX

       "worn smooth through years of contact with
the sand and grease of the mind"

                "strings
treasures of perfomation"

          "customizes
an exercise in patience"

x

"and when asked what threads together abstraction and the puppets"

"my voices"

"she says at the same time"

XI

      "i am responsible
for providing the roof for my sister
as well as for me. we have no home
at all. i cannot just leave her
and go. i live in my car
virtually. i love her"

                        "we (the family group)
were scattered abroad more than once"

                        "i'm the other,
the sister on a negative journey. whose third eye
will swerve to advertise
round worlds"

XII

        "staring with rigid attention an owl
that waits for menaced endings"

                      "two blue arms
curve out. hesitate. as if to catch
a viper serrating air"

                        "they cut
loaves of bread with three grains of sand
fuse beginnings"

XIII

       "the fine force moving you
with unrepeatability. embrace it let it
go that you don't suffocate it
you"

               "everywhere
in my eyes my ears hands and memory. in every
breath"

                "if an image
answers excluding another answer the question is
crushed"

XIV

"from, politicization, provocation, a pain"

"exasperated.
and excitable. a policy in spite"

•

"of
inherbitions. the gift of being
wounded"

XV

        "armed"

                              "she sleeps with
arms embracing openness"

"some treasure
buried
lost
forgotten"

XVI

      "the gopher may not hear its own
hissed shape"

                                  "of eyes narrate"

    "mines opened to metamorphosis
from pine to blue spruce"

XVII

      "i've seen your messengers of winter.
three fangs lacquered in their throats. the gorge
over us"

                                        "my thoughts went"

          "to larks' spurs"

XVIII

      "with no object to"

                                        "critical temperatures
when you coils their thoughts together color"

        "what's left"

XIX

      "the studied hide elated eyes in narrow
openings. strong as enough"

                            "the eusocial
roll up yous in a ball of leavetakings"

              "me educated in dust and matter
at the moving edge of sharpness"

XX

"this blue is nothing but also green, colour impeccable"

"colour skin,
the south wind, an extension of solid"

"colour to complement oxygen
in an allusive fecundity"

XXI

    "at frontiers"

                          "blade and flower"

                          "and feathered armor for"

XXII

      "as beads"

                                       "a work is as precious
as the love it witnesses. a sense of measure and
a profound sense. lines which are like straight lines
in motion. the pathos inseparable from all real life"

                                          "passing gently behind
things lifted translocated not to forget
respect. facultation"

XXIII

       "how lines and divisions are created"

                             "how islands
are cut off by the sea"

                                 "how stones
are carved by hand memory"

XXIV

"incured"

"her search through
feared and loose symbols"

"last night
he dreamt of blue snakes"

XXV

"this blue is nothing but also green"

                                           "colour
layered upon layer upon layers of her leaking
now
through hard infinities"

"anguished is a reality starved of yearning zones"

XXVI

      "she sets her thoughts,"

                                        "dwellings for transitives,"

  "in a silver horizon"

XXVII

      "writing to alter.
the grammars they create towards
an encounter. writing intimates.
writing in tensed. a cunning matrix
of poem fervid and almost"

                                          "cracks.
                                        facets."

            "relationship of center to
outside"

XXVIII

      "architect of notes. renouncing certain rules by inventing some. dwellings that translate to the sea, spandrelled. perused. dwellings for people. drifting faces"

                                        "another garment"

            "please excuse the blue envelope"

                            .

XXIX

       "there were times she was inspired
by the shape of the tools alone"

                         "filling cracks
like blue fills losses"

          "you can't really climb
into somebody else's dream"

xxx

        "this artist, who says, i love
structure
      ritual
            patterns"

                      "edgezones"

            "at night we don't lie"

.

XXXI

    "i'm looking outward and inward"

                            "alternating women"

                "women who were looking both inward and outward"

XXXII

       "eyes graticuled like sand crypts"

                             "to follow
the heartline"

                         "there is one route
to the sea and one route to the snow and they are
the same route"

XXXIII

    "how to find the winds fallen from
the walls of a phenomenal sky? how to reconnect
auricle and still song? how in the diminishing distance
to apprehend terminal growth and pollen grain?"

                              "the past
                              (she knew)
                              was the future"

                              "there is no
                              arriving there
                              is only paths"

hathor in egypt

damage

        in response to a perceived threat to their liveliness
              certain cobras can spit venom
                   some metres
          as a fine spray directed at the intruder's eyes
                causing intense pain
                    sometimes
                  a loss of sight

                     o   o   o

    skin is the hidden
    touch it might be mashed
    by the maces of control

                                    the cicatrice
                                    is a lifemark,
                                    for future vision

a sparrow is
passion, migrant
of rusted tracts

obstacle

      order of the squamous
      redesignated serpents
            order of
         scale and gloss
sufficient unto their tongues
        horizontal tree
   branches held together
by the bootstraps of naturalists

        o   o   o

in the beginning
a thread of flax
on a loom

                                      name
                                      adjusted to
                                      the jar

an upper and lower paths meet
at an obtuse memory of
patterns hidden in unfired sand

self

       the skin is shed in one piece
            at intervals
         the eyes turn blue
       like cloud-rubbed stones
          the tail points
           to departure
         inside-outwards

            o   o   o

between navel
and jaw a heart
and death-blue jewel

                          born
                          for
                          her

it is a loaf of
if leavened with
your senses

divide

tongue deep split for sense of direction

o o o

do not quail at the attempt
to collect and return
the ideas in our chromosomes

                                            to draw a line like
                                            a carpenter scoring
                                            the heartwood

to
share
air

imprison

with a web of powerful muscles
snakes undulate crawl sidewind
and concertina through space
they are necessarily
secretive and evasive
in captivity
potential atrophies

o   o   o

we have domesticated
fire to flickering
in a vacuum

                                                        broken
                                                        sticks and
                                                        styles

                mind caught
                in the noose of
                the mouth

think

snake stories have radiated to inhabit nearly all global niches
arid deserts
thin
⁌ and luxuriant forests
disorder of water
but not the coldest

 o o o

    the hand draws, the language
    encrypts, the signs touch
    the limping eye

                                  naked edge, naked
                                  suggestions, hands,
                                  abandoned gestures

          memory,
          my dented range,
          my pencil's errand

                say

    still in its own hiss

          o   o   o

wearing
vitreous
rings

                        now
                        at the joining of
                        ahead and

        performance
        sintered agents
        directed motion

provisions

the scales of a desert horned viper are coloured and patterned
like their shifting carpet of sand
beneath which
the snake burrows by shuffling
until
just eyes and horns
break the surface

o   o   o

a broken river of
english flowed now
across her dreams

                                            a broken raft of
                                            thinking flowed
                                            now out of them

                        a paste in
                        faint seens
                        she spreads on broken bread

relate

      the most dangerous
   depends on an interpretation
          perhaps
       the inland taipan
      if most is chemical
          unknown
          if most
         numerical

             o   o   o

warped
from
past

to   the crafthand
wefted,   must not slip,
there to there   laying in

                              night applied
                              with jasmine,
                              hazy jet

ointment

      a few species polish their skins
      with a clear fast-drying liquid
      they secrete through the nose

          o   o   o

too young to touch
the alabaster ghosts,
the alkaline forms

                            to mix natron
                            with jade, to heal
                            with a jest

                            or a spelling
                            smeared from a pot
                            of false gold

leaf

the scales are folded dermis
epidermis
the outer layers
scales will not detach
without hurting the skin
outer
and inner surfaces
a hinge
smooth
or
keeled pitted tubercled
scales for protection
and flexibility
scales of caution
and cryptic colours

o   o   o

lines of numbed magic
use it as tissue to,
invest with silence

what the mouth can see,
codes of bright autumn,
yellow thoughts reliefed

on brazen,
and the sound of
a distance falling

incite

a fitting death for a herpetologist

o   o   o

       she wears a collar
       of blue
       randomness

rings
of
sequence

    her footprints in the sand
    fill
    with the shadows of knives

small

        live young
    a few or very many
          or eggs
   reproductive strategies
for how to invest in memory

          o   o   o

without a waterdrop
no wave
ripple or eddy

scentlines
diffusing between
warped and shot

    a palimpsest of
    salt soul
    and error

eternity

      it has evolved several times
            viviparous
          born colubrid
          with vast eyes
           born viper
        with hinged fangs

            o   o   o

    number by a jab of again,
    heartwear as jeopardised by
    pure enzymes, and again numbed à jamais

time iced with ritual,
orient your zest axis,
may need sugar

        finding a dune's shadow
        she begins to sort
        the grains of sand

hear

        their blue is nothing but also
        bent
        science being an effort to see
        the hidden
        inventing languages
        fragmenting skeleton and flesh
        into words
        snakes have no external ears
        they hear through their body
        vibrations from ground to bone

        o   o   o

        the harp the lyre the lute
        whose strings have been plucked
        by time

collection
of brittle
rattles

              but not one
              written note
              of their music

deep

some snakes lay their eggs in the cavities of trees
some lay them in the nests of alligators
or termites
some dig their own nests
in soft ground
some
choose coral caves

o   o   o

        she saddled time in a stable
        propped
        on a foundation of dreams

she inhaled
her mare's
breath

                time
                plunged
                into perhaps

wing

call it help
or coercion
blindsnake and screech-owl
nestlings plagued
by parasites
the owl brings the snake
to a larval feast

o   o   o

night arms its jangles,
the hectic air,
dance of self and jetsam

one could write like a worrier
of whispering waste
woundwashed

write through the wax wind
on white walls
waiting towards

write in water
at wildest wavelengths
words for weaning

with a wick
twisted from
my eyelashes

sea

      their blue is nothing but also bent
                    light
  scattered by a stack of purine crystals
              blue a skin
           and blue a sky
    the fourth power of wavelength

              o   o   o

    this blue
    is nothing
    but also salt

swallow histories
run down the roof
of her mouth

                    over the swimming pool
                    of gods

child

    learn a world mapped by molecules
            coordinate
       in pungency and perfume

            o   o   o

  this blue
  is nothing
  but also self

to understand that the future could retreat
from an envy of
anteriors

                          . . .
                          . . .
                          . . .

pupil

most snakes move the lens backwards and forwards
as in a camera
what they cannot define sharply
they see shiver flicker or tremble
on every side
round vertical or horizontal

o   o   o

        her right night eye,
        ajar to clipped angels,
        hall for the jettisoned

her right nascent eye
so that jackals might wander into her dreams
with the dead in time

                                    a ceramic stare
                                    a ceramic stained
                                    with empyred soot
                                    a ceramic fourthrite

adhere

                for support
snakes erect their heads by expanding elongated ribs
                       transfer
               dorsal markings
        or bright and contrasting patterns
                   and observe
      that hood markings are only found
           where humans revere cobras

                          o   o   o

    transfer,
    the heat of these fingers to the dough
    sticking to them

observe,
those warp threads stretched straight between
the uprights of a loom

follow,
that silent music
empalmed by the chironomists

words

species
our goals and values?
are we going to appreciate other
animals as they are
mutually adjusting

o   o   o

"may your words occur
may your magic shine
give breath to her whose throat is constricted"

"may your words occur
may your magic shine
truly effective — (proved) millions of times"

"may your words occur
may your magic shine
writing causes them to be remembered"

charcoal

from burning organic matter in limited air
burning of
wood date stones and bones
pure amorphous carbon
used in gunpowder and cartooning
respirators
because
reactive and highly porous
fragile life
with one lung

o   o   o

infinitely black,
the eighth refraction
of the rainbow

the nightingale adjusting
junctions along
halls of jealousy

    after roads of chariots and tanks
    footprints converge
    at the limits of ash

brightness

mimicry is very widespread among snakes
(not to mention those that feign death
in the presence of a threat)
snakes as mimic and model
(müller)
as model or mimic
(bates)

o   o   o

    this blue
    is nothing
    but also glaze

mysterious
as
copper efflorescence

    question
    whose answer may not be
    illumination

storm

i don't catch them
he replied
mambas
whose heads have been described as
coffin shaped
spasms

    o   o   o

    the seasons of today
    lost
    in meteorological time

to control at last
because the barometer is rising
into the air

        to control at last,
        but the rising air
        strikes

fat

    attack with the speed of humour
      digest with a metabolism
        tuned to need

        o   o   o

    the nature of these mitochondria in thighs
    heart and mind to play jazz
    slow with saturated ideas

haste is for the jet-lagged
natural esters of phrases
ontogenising perception

          narrative options
          earth erupting
          like a pustule in space

fresh

     her blue is nothing but also
                tongue
   the effort of the den to escape
         being cemented
                  in
      (*she is beautiful in youth*)
           dynamited
           the rattler
           a free sign

        o   o   o

these
are the ciphers
and sounds

that will perish
with us
this

                the passage of paper
                into rudiments
                of soul

seek

their chambers split by double membranes
pits between the vipers' nostril and eye
infrasense the heat of life
in our darkness

      o   o   o

a necessary
but not adequate
condition

*(the very exigencies
of materiality,
the susceptibility of the world*

to injury) justice also
in the heart of
a sunflower

perceive

    and the fossil documents
    a rich record of speciation
        and extinction
        among cobras

        o   o   o

    efflorescent
    effective
    effarant

    effleuraged
    english
    as foreign at the fingertips

a needle
threaded with papyrus roots and flux
mending

                the nets of time
                nine hebrew loops
                one whorl

flame

      once joined difficult to separate
               his hemipenis
              his mating plug
           her storage of sperm

              o   o   o

     under gauze
     the migration of cells
     pseudopods

a cobalt trace
a brand of delicate
dedifferentiation

                              burns
                              scars
                              grafts

green

            charmed
  by the shadow of a vinesnake
the parrotsnake weaving through a palm fronb
      the pitviper hanging by its tail
           from a petiole
           charmed
     by the effort to generate

               o   o   o

    salts of copper
    yellow mixed with blue
    complement to red

  the pigment of energy synthesis
  reflecting surplus
  back to us

  the peel of an apple
  thin shade in a pistachio nut
  rush sign

  not available dye
  just a haze
  for the jaded eye

when languages do not distinguish them
the waves dance in silence
in polychromatic patterns

of knowledge

rage

somewhere in their tails
the synthesis of foul scents
discharged as spray
smeared on themselves
or on us
do we love
what we learn?

o   o   o

hathor
goddess of music and disorder
re's daughter

mistress of scintillance
our lady of punt
a usurper

just as a breeze can topple into a storm
a hand can hit what it would caress
to cow and to cobra

break

    snakes cannot climb up their own cladogram
        because the branches flow
           from west to east
            unfused smile
          desert mona lisas
         retrieval of the lost
       from the tomb of memory

          o   o   o

    one cannot embroider a dress without
    breaking the thread, breaking the thread
    does not destroy the pattern

does not complete it
does not obligate it
breaking the thread is only

to breathe
respirer
atmen

anilineated dreams

’1111

       near the day
the scapegoats are slaughtered.   near the hour
their houses burn down. near the moment
hymens are sabred.   pesach

                        <   o   o

    a cloth
finer than we can weave.   perhaps
a finer-fibred flax.   perhaps urine
to reduce their vats.   eaux nils   (excrement)

                        <   o   o

             sublimate
of a photograph.   a robe bright
as a field of rape.   she reaps camel dung
to sell as fuel.   leben

'1121

           to where years
are force-fed down
enraged throats,   (infants
buried alive),   because
she is she,   no abstract

                    o   <   o

       a twisted fibril
of microstories,   leaves
on tussled water, a twisted
fibril,   lost
to us   (detained)

                    o   <   o

                emerging
like a strand of hennaed hair, (oboe
or clarinet?), from orchestral dusk, a note
spared

'1201

      exhausted then
on the north side of futurism. electric
dread.   noughts. prayers

                   >   o   >

      the low heritability
of flags and crosses. bolted
flowers. drought. water   (garden)

                   >   o   >

                the last german writer
in the city of kafka. an almond
draught.   home. elsewhere

'1211

    this blue is nothing but also
ice, motionless, sharp flint, on all four sides, *rest*
— *Silence*, enclosure in a floating darkness, enclosure
in the pride of civilisation, enclosure in relationships
destroyed by a manufractured environment

      o o o

   this blue is nothing but also
style, or petal, or
seed, or filament, or
stigma, recombination
of editions, recombination on
the arms of a chromosome, recombination
within the metaphasic fields
of laxity
& axiom (moon)

      o o o

       this blue is nothing
but also mark, deserted seas, tone
scrape, bleeding triptychs, skyless
skies, an enterprise after
the silence, an enterprise after
the manner of patriarchs, an enterprise
after materiologies resisting all dissolution

'1221

        this blue is nothing but also
blood,   this landscape of corpses
refusing burial.   memory of a black
monastery.   reliefs of flower & fruit &
fable. no relief.   the house abandoned
to the wind.   the lake
that vanished.   and then the poet
writing
there is no dictionary
with words for these terrors

                <   >   o

    this blue is nothing but
uniform, the war a cutting off
of synthetic supplies.   the brief recovery
of natural dye.   the reprieve
of colonial habits.   history.   waist deep
into the devil's tank.   beating the liquid. if not
death then they wrote cancer impotence headaches
and temporary blindness   (clothing)

                <   >   o

                    a pencil
rues over the surface,   the soil
tilled by sharp instruments
waits for seed.   hidden light
germinates in erasure.   charred ghosts
collect ashes for their loved ones.   drops
of rain.   your eye keeps crawling
on yonder.   your past
is reframed.   he wrote he would destroy
confinement of inert walls *to achieve*

                         fluidity

'2001

              at dusk two old men find
the deadnettles. the bindweed,   make camp
in a circle of thistles,   sit and watch,   a dance
of grass seed.   mattress
of camomile.   pillow
of mustard.   they reminisce along red-edged
polygons.   their solace as the numbers fill the night
with green shadows. this
is a common journey

                         >   o   <

         a thoughtline
of nubian musicians.   blind
harpist,   she can only touch
an arch of time,   the strings
sing,   where the mouth
is muted.   attached
to memory.   between cataracts.   a
cut language glows through alabaster
walls.   the dancers from the past
and the dancers without
patterns.   the beauty and the beaten   (mourn)

                         >   o   <

                             inside
the penalty of our species.   you
again,   you understand the interior,   dim
idea,   soul and the heart thrown in. a day
of blue faces.   but
some nights you dance.   sometimes
in a narrow ribbon of yellow.   then
you have the dimensions of a storm whose feet may
pass.   that way you may scramble through

'2011

        signs
are reinvested by history. the left-hand path
is swallowed by shadows.   or infinity.   the future
baptised in a disguised light.   the secret
is vehemently reassigned. hate-crossed

                >   o   o

        if lines could live
in their hesitations.   if arms
could embrace
the body of air.   because
i see birds,   vultures flying
in deep-grey formations.   i see
words
surrounding what
is hidden.   hectic   (magic)

                >   o   o

the net is open
by definition.   the vision of the web
is fugitive.   i'm sending them back,   the princess
and three rotten oranges.   i'm weaving my signs
into the curtain.   helixed

           into the night
of street walkers, into the flaws of their cities
cloaked in black velvet. an artist of dreams suited in
rhapsodic green with a buttonholed sprig of red
ampersands. a dictator of the lost
future of history tears of lead shot
from sharp eyes. return to near the
place, one-choice-or-another

                 o   <   <

            the crop is pulled
rather than cut,   and may be left in the field
to be retted by dew.   microbes then digest
the pectic materials cementing fibres
to surrounding tissues. like a reading digests
the poetic materials cementing signed to sign.   a
vulture has landed,   time in the grip of flu   (rot)

                 o   <   <

         too many clothes
for one suitcase,   and we got lost
on the longest road
to the airport.   everyone exclaims
the neatness of my handwriting
but how many see
the turquoise shadows? each morning
her face is different
sometimes a passionflower
tattoed on her cheek.   or eyes
as deep as silt,   or lips
sore with hunger

'2101

        the mimicry of birds,   paralysis
of drifting space,   passenger and pilot
travelling to a scheduled place,   silk scarves
and tickertape. biplanes.   jets.   bombers.   for if
a picture is worth a thousand words maybe a poem
can paint a thousand pictures and perhaps
this is not a poem

                                   <   o   <

        an alluvial plan,   substitute
for infinity.   the whip of the sea whip of the air
whip of the land,   necklace of foam
beads.   fluxion.   birds.   paper.   for if
you follow the shore for a day
you might find a village of astronomers
drawing constellations in the sand   (delta)

                                   <   o   <

     from the dull to sparkling,   every word
and its translations.   between the spontaneous and
the deliberate,   the match of chance
and control. premise.   pause.   practice.   for if
the future asks the poem the reasons for an absence
of names in a period that had not yet
lost property

'2111

        the hands cup and gather
a notionful of the ocean.　dip
and hold.　　an illegal
prayer.　　the water evaporates only
as its bonds break incensed by
an imperious sun.　　naked claims. millions of them

                >　　>　　>

        flax waste bleached and ground
is used to make paper
for banknotes.　cut
and dry.　　to prepare
the corpses.　　i had a supervisor
whose household task
was making bread
he said absorbed
aggression.　　pound of flesh. mortal resistance　　(salt)

                >　　>　　>

        a charity is funding
fresh attempts
to counter it.　war
and more.　　epidemic
violence.　　i have to translate
our duty not to
listen to a social science
of ambivalence.　　on being. disobedient

        they come
half out of a river of stones
half in a nexus of nothing.   leakiness
of again,   pardons pinned to
nowhere. a violence that tests
the test.   no zones,   the individual
destroyed in returns to singularity

<   o   +

            and also to wrap around
cigarettes and cover the cracks
in walls. faulty restorations, columns
filled with rubble. varicosed views
of culture. passed on, ethical refusals
to domicile estimated customs   (child)

<   o   +

              a century that saw
the triumph of the image
over language?   a movement
of poets,   museum
of painters.   the safety
of idiom.   as if,   as if
i too had built a glass-walled mind
around a cedar tree

'2201

        prelude
to horror. the gas
and the gaze. the scream
and the shivering. the silence
and the explosions

                o   <   >

        flexible axes.   the bread
and the pain. the covert and
the judgement.   the air and the
aspidistra   (throat)

                o   <   >

                on
prerogatives. first she says   .
one thing.   then she
scatters her matter. but she always buys
blue roses

'2211

<   +

   linseed oil is used in making paint
varnish and pharmaceuticals, the seeds
are crushed for cattle feed, used in
trial and time issues in mundane
and moral. airwave power. control tower. the lost
arm of the laws (and)

<   +

    the beats of a lament
take the darkness between home
and genesis, batterings rush to
quietness, silence crossed with thing
struggle to conceive
in going. violins. viola. imperfectly quartet

'2 2 2 1

<

<

                             the when
of a world not to forget this.   the when of
a world drawn by the others.   the when of a
world of lacquered roses. the when of a world
between two commas.   the
when in the world.   when

''0001

"0011

        future,
what words will do in the future
they wrote.   a venue in risk.
   she'll come

                >   <   o

        a pledge,   digging into siltwords
with a curved gaze. to whittle
to woo.   doubled   (behold)

                >   <   o

                          city,
  a body of enclosed
and rupture lines.   remembered futures.
   graffics

''0021

        this blue is nothing but also
flame,   the wick is a tree and the fuel
is the skin of soldiers.   coconut oil.
   fatty acids.   aluminium. crematogen.
  napalm.   she goes north towards a river
she goes south towards a sea.
     captured by morning.   calm

                < o >

        this blue is nothing but also
fast,   even as it fades its hue remains
unforgettable.   like a dancer.   like
a mermaid.   who has sold her tongue.
   and her sisters.   their hair.   the flame
in the alabaster bowl feeds on
oxymorons.   united nations.   dome   (festival)

                < o >

this blue is nothing but also
glass, a deep blue vessel
balanced in the hands of a blind man.
   at a party.   a crowded room.   somewhere
underground.   smoke and red light.
    silence.   then
the blind man runs his finger round the rim of
the blue bowl.   unwritten music. mine

''0101

        she passes through a toll gate in the east
and up with the wind to arrive
at a dew line.   and it is frozen.
  she finds an angel with
your wings.   a stone
littered with light.

                      <   <   >

                this is that
which came forth from my hand
and what i rubbed into my fingers
from a vulva.   the line encircles.
  the dancer wears a hiking boot.
      the binding grows looser   (ritual book)

                      <   <   >

    i built this temporary altar
for the 12th anniversary
of a mother's death.
  three damask roses.
    photograph
and one red candle.
  then i drank
two blue moons

"0111

        trial.
drama.   dragon.   dormant.
dramaticity.   damascened.
  dropsy.   drowsiness.   dramamine.   she
scrapes a piece of her placenta
and carries it in her body

              o   >   >

        line.
inspire.   inspread.   eyespot.   in the
spume of it.   implicate.
    in-place.   in the
head. in
spangles.
 persons create the illusion
that they are not mere referents of   (lock of hair)

              o   >   >

        mould.
 cold pink. collect.   crassness.   cold wars
in the house.   cede the past.   corny.
    discontent. coldheaded. saved by a laugh
as vast as
a door into a room of daily lives

''0121

    she continues
in gorges. she consumes
with the greed of uncertainty.
 at a singular and plural pace, she collects
life amplified by standard errors of replication

       o > <

    what we eat
leaves us
as heat.
 the ungorgeous
swollen with
deficiency.
 the lips
an ellipse of
erasure.
 defined by
a hand germinating from the mouth
or deserted fields (hunger)

       o > <

    rescued by an aquiline.
  rescued by sagittal communication.
 rescued by a delphic nursery,
   rescued by consolation in a constellation of
cornflowers

"0201

        guided missiles
and misguided men, poetry
might remind of richness and diversity.
    murderless thoughts. the housewife

                    >   <   >

        this blue is nothing
but also love,
   but the flame in the mouth
scours unsaturated clauses.
  rêves après.   im nachthaus   (night)

                    >   <   >

        she says she eats
memory and moths, because
if you open your eyes you can look at the dark.
   now close them.
  open them

"0211

            in a veil of peppermint.
she hides,
   not faith and politics.
burnt flesh

               >   o   +

            child on tram
twists her brown hair. father,
 leans against the window.
 they tease   (embrace)

               >   o   +

                 when there are no more commas.
   she drinks,   peppermint tea
and tears. one note

"0221

                  she hears someone
on the other side of the moon.   she digs
for stardust in a flooded garden. sews a corpse
to a carol.   advancing and retreating
to protect an anonymous nature

                              <   <   <

                  she braids a biography
from both sides of now.   mixes sea-spray and ash
in a jar of how. her death's a dress
she cannot recall.   putting her hand to her mouth
she pulls out a space
where others say
all   (sing)

                              <   <   <

                  she wears
successful shoes
and a bright-pink apron.   her eyes caress
strangeness in soft shades of brown. her ring she recycles
from her self.   she wants to write an opera
whose hero isn't killed
by a rose thorn

"1001

      she meets her other sister again,
  whose eyes are as square as television screens,
the pupils round as bullet holes,
  the past and a past
touch

<   >   >

        this blue is nothing but also
squeezed, the white shadow of winter's hand
on the pulse,   borrowed from a spider's web,
 eyelids of angels   (wing)

<   >   >

         this blue is nothing
but also sky,
 (when i remember to look at it),
  wide as my serenity,
and as transient

                        on the path between
school and university.
  can we save the elm trees,
      can we not
give up? on the forest path between railway station
and research station my head broke
into sunlight

                    >   <   <

                    customers still prefer
the bleached or white product.   but dyes
are coming in. perhaps light
and pause.   perhaps where the pencil cannot
hesitate to nominate the omissions
the print wipes out   (plunder)

                    >   <   <

                                but my body
walked on in a loose coat of mist.   alone
now and
later, (orchids and orchid).   but
in that autumn
the commissioned trees stood
like giant dandelions
dispersing tufts of light

''1021

        innate. acquired.
    resistance.   T cells.   B cells.
         killer cells.   proliferation of
terms
fragmenting our bodies.
                  health,
        immunity
to certain predicitions.   dis-
ease.   or-self.   world
of other anticipations.
    my history complex.
  exoned

               >   >   o

            fragment. borders.   of blue
stripes.   fragments.   of
state.   mummy cloths.   preserved
by climate
& sand
& burial customs.
                  bread,
       the invariant need
for nourishment.
    to go.
   or stretch,
  invert the gravity of
idea.   the answer is
without. perchance   (perish)

             >   >   o

                       planets.
  orbits.   sun
system.   the selves.
   others.   some

system.   analogy
exchanging parts
for universals.   words,
    exist
to segregate and conjugate.   to
cleave.   mutate.   micro-ornamenting
abstraction.   almost to
distraction.   two cleaves

"1101

        this blue
migrates like a metaphor,
  like promises in a dyadic field,
  like a denatured protest,
  as far as its mass will allow

                o   >   +

            writing
to link unmentionables, writing
wrapped in where it wasn't wanted,
    writing
at the erotic, wickerwork
with a her handle   (offer)

                o   >   +

it can be both terse and lyrical,
  an analytical and precise mind,
  though was she mad at the end,
    of the influence of silence

"1111

        she is covered in stories
and tired of.
  (nastic dancing.
 needful dreaming.
  nowly dying)

        <   >   +

        linen is confined
to top-market outlets.
 i am the dream.
  miracle dancer.
die disfigured   (count)

        <   >   +

  then glitter fell out of
torn shoes and a hiccup.
 rose-blue dreamers.
 kennst du den tanz?
  loyal to death

     now they hear the restless whispers,
   amplified by silence,
  the swallowed words released from
exhausted parentheses,
   grandmother and mother merging in
the absence of myth

        < > <

       if synthetic fibres shrivel,
  as oil resources shrink,
   she took a jar and filled it with
lines falling from blue lips,
  she sat in a café
unwinding
the fashion for black (turn back)

        < > <

     trumpet trumpet trumpet
piano, tamtam tamtam
voice,
  the prayer builds a nest of echoes
in a flowering ear,
   how can a student learn of
what the teachers cannot hear

"1201

      the film dissolves
into brighter colours. in the lab
the viruses take off their coats.
a longing for order. of angels
                    avatars
                                  anorexics

           o   >   o

              this blue
has also been called upon to lie.
 in the fields the tobacco was flowering.
   the sprinklers were sprinkling. the bees
were not buzzing and no birds sang   (phallus)

           o   >   o

       i climbed a ladder
of champagne bottles.   five hands
had to help me when i reached the top.
   i am a large woman.   i did this
because i wanted a part

"1211

       brückenscherben,
durch eine zeitschaft,
unter anderen.
lügt die dichterin in der nichtmuttersprache

           o   <   +

          though it creases,
  fancy knits hide flaws.
 an egg for breakfast.   a flock of words lifting
for winter migration   (gather)

          o   <   +

        une île du sel,
 un vent incessant.
   une église sans toit.
    personne n'y sait s'habituée
sans rêve et cor

''1 2 2 1

    this word is nothing
in the rainbow but a blue passed
from mouth to eye, a passage painted
on the facestone of the sky, as one by one
the raindrops gather dust in their own falling,
 from one grave to another,
   another scream,
    to live beyond

         < < o

       this blue is nothing but also
pearl
in a list between
milk
and hell,
   dip again
for a note
antidote to jangles,
   twice more
for a thought
flying on its back across water,
 dip
into the bowl
and bend, twist
in a rhyme,
   deduce the cheek (vexed)

         < < o

        the voyage begins in the middle
and ends in the middle of it, the exclusive middle
of apprehension, (no not even the scream
just the impossible sign
for it), from one science
to cymbals, moon-dried music,
wake in lyric

''2001

winter has arrived,   day of shortest day
when a soprano,   lending more than
to sisters out of time,
     cuts stencils in ice

          o   o   <

          .   from a frowning heart,
                    along a rough track
               from a frowning heart,
                    along a rough track
               from a frowning heart,
                    along a rough track   (beauty)

          o   o   <

                    bound to see edges,
                         pruning limes
                    in a garden of alleys,
                      to leave more
                    by borrowing a pink horse,
                         than to shy
                    to move